A CHRISTIAN IN INDIA

Lessons from a Seminarian who Discovers Jesus in Hindu Temples

Cescilio Chavez, Ph.D.

Bladensburg, MD

A Christian in India

Published by
Inscript Books
a division of Dove Christian Publishers
P.O. Box 611
Bladensburg, MD 20710-0611
www.dovechristianpublishers.com

Copyright © 2020 by Cescilio Chavez

Cover Design by Nadia Chatsworth

ISBN: 978-1-7348625-6-0

Library of Congress Control No. 2020943807

All rights reserved. No part of this publication may be used or reproduced without permission of the publisher, except for brief quotes for scholarly use, reviews or articles.

Published in the United States of America

25 24 23 22 21 20   1 2 3 4 5

Dedication

This, my first book, is dedicated to my mother, Virginia Briseño Chavez, who not only shaped my moral compass but also represented all that is beneficent which directly speaks to the ultimate power of our panentheistic God, who daily continues to manifests Himself in our lives.

My mother reminded us nightly of our ultimate authority.

Hasta mañana amá.

Si Dios quiere!

On our birthdays a mere "Happy Birthday" would not suffice. Instead, my mother evoked the blessings of our overseer with "Que Dios te quarde muchos años."

These and many other words continue today to unravel the mystery and beauty of my God.

Gracias Amá.

Contents

Acknowledgments vii
Introduction ix

I
Arrival — New Delhi Neighborhood 3

II
Explorimg the Neighborhood 5

III
The Taj Mahal 10

IV
Birla Temple 14

V
Gurudwara Bangla Sahib Temple, Lotus Temple 19

VI
ISKCON Temple, Swaminarayan Akshardham Temple 24

VII
Tera Manzil, The Himalayas, Haridwar: The Holy Ganges 29

VIII
Mathura 39

IX
St. Anthony's Secondary School 53

X
Mother Teresa's Missionaries of Charity Jeevan Jyoti Home 56

Conclusion 59
About the Author 64
Works Consulted 65

Acknowledgments

Foremost, I would like to thank my mentor, Dr. Ruben Habito, Professor of World Religions at Southern Methodist University's Perkins School of Theology in Dallas, Texas. His willingness to share his knowledge of the world with his seminary students and his guidance throughout my endeavor is priceless. By teaching me about inclusivism and pluralism, he allowed my illumination to occur. Secondly, I would like to thank Dr. Craig. C. Hill, Dean of the Perkins School of Theology and a New Testament Scholar, for his graceful "green light" on this project.

I also wish to thank my parents and siblings for their role modeling of good Christian people. I love them and could not imagine living with any other family. Finally, I wish to thank my Perkins family of fellow seminarians; together we grow and learn about and with the Word of Jesus Christ. God be with you always.

Introduction

Growing up Catholic in San Antonio, Texas, I lived with all the Catholic tenets. My family and I believed in and lived by the Ten Commandments. We attended mass, received Baptism, believed and practiced the seven sacraments and the twelve articles of the Catholic faith, went to confession at least once a year, received Holy Communion, and believed in the Holy Trinity; we observed days of fasting and abstinence (Lent and Ash Wednesday) and provided the church whatever help we could possibly afford.

In 2017, while taking my first religion class (World Religions) as a seminarian at the Perkins School of Theology at Southern Methodist University in Dallas, Texas, I became much more interested in a "universal God." Was Jesus a universal God? In class, our professor, Dr. Ruben Habito, led us in very lively discussions on Buddhism, Hinduism, Islam, and other world religions. I recall my statement at the beginning of my first semester: "I am taking this class so that I may more deeply understand who my God is."

While future classes taken as a seminarian shed much light into Christianity, such as the Council of Trent, The First Lateran, Erasmus, The Reformation, the New Testament, and learning about various concepts of faith, no experience would prove as enlightening and illuminating as my travel to India. Between my desire to learn more about my Christianity and my aspiration to learn other religions, God afforded me a fateful opportunity to search for my God in the Hindu religion.

In this book, I will chronicle my attempt to understand how Jesus and God relate to Hindu or if Christianity relates to Hindu at all. To discover this, I needed to approach this question from a much different perspective than a Christian one. The lasting history of Christianity is attributed to many things. But foremost, I believe Christianity has endured because it is something more than itself. My question was not a simple one. Thus, it would take a not-so-simple approach. The need to answer this question had to come from within me. But to do so, I had to look outward and "be" outward. I did not go to India to investigate or research Hinduism. I went to India to understand Christianity better. I had never been to India nor have I been a student of Hinduism other than to have a brief introduction to it in my first year in Perkins Seminary. After a week in India, I began to see myself in a way I had never seen before. I was beginning to see Hinduism from a Christian perspective while also understanding Christianity from a Hindu point of view. Was I to create my own religious world? I do not attempt to compare or contrast or categorize Christianity and Hinduism. For to do so would be futile indeed.

While I understand that books (once published) become their own identity, it is also important to comprehend that writing this book began in India from notes I took in a notebook, on toilet paper, on restaurant napkins, or whatever else I could find to write on. I would like you to not only read it but stop once in a while to digest what I have experienced, to contemplate what was just read (chapter by chapter or sentence by sentence) to consider whether it connects with you spiritually or intellectually. This book is not meant to be authoritative by any means. But it is written from my heart to express and share my religious growth. To read anything for the sake of reading it is pointless. There exists enough futility of religious knowledge in this world as it is. "Give ear to my words, O

Lord, consider my meditation" (Psalm 5:1 AKJV). Perhaps Gandhi expressed it best when he said:

> "I write just as the Spirit moves me at the time of writing. I do not claim to know definitely that all conscious thought and action on my part is directed by the Spirit. But on examination of the greatest steps that I have taken in my life, as also of those that may be regarded as the least, I think it will not be improper to say that all of them were directed by the Spirit. It is perhaps now somewhat easy to understand why I believe that I am writing this story as the Spirit prompts me" (Experiments with Truth Audiobook 2009).

I had no special preparation or training for a spiritual quest or pilgrimage. I am a simple person who wanted to take on a not-so-simple question. That one question took me from one end of this planet to the other end. Would I succeed in answering my question? Gandhi once said, "If I have the belief that I can do it, I shall surely acquire the capacity to do it even if I may not have it at the beginning."

> "Preserve me, O God: For in thee do I put my trust" (Psalm 16:1 AKJV).

Swami Vivekananda stated:

> Take up one idea. Make that one idea our life; dream of it; think of it; live on that idea. Let the brain, the body, muscle, nerves, every part of your body be full of that idea, and just leave every other idea alone. This is the way to success, and this is the way great spiritual giants are produced.

First, it is important to understand that Hinduism represents an accepted term, but, more adequately, Hinduism represents an umbrella term that includes many religions or a family of religions. For example, Hindu devotees may follow only Lord Shiva or only Lord Vishnu or they may belong to a community dedicated to a specific deity. One can discern what deity one is a follower of by the tilaka on a Hindu's forehead. Tilakas vary in their marking styles and their color.

About ninety-five percent of Hindus live in India. Others live mostly in areas adjacent to India, such as Nepal, where Hinduism stands as the official state religion. India does not have an official state religion. India prides itself on being the world's largest democracy.

Additionally, there are many similarities between Christianity and Hinduism; for example, the belief in life after death. Christians believe in eternity in Heaven (or Hell) and, in some cases, purgatory. Hindus believe in a constant cycle of reincarnation until one reaches enlightenment. The practices of Christianity include prayer, worship in churches or cathedrals, and, in some branches, sacraments. Hindus practice meditation, yoga, yajna (communal worship), and offerings in a temple. Christians believe in one God (monotheism), Father, Son, Holy Spirit (Holy Trinity). Hindus believe in many gods and goddesses but realize that they all originate from Atman (soul, self). Christians believe that the means to salvation lies in one's belief in Jesus Christ's passion, death, and resurrection. Hindus believe that the means to salvation is by reaching enlightenment via the path of knowledge, devotion, and the path of good deeds. The scriptures of Christians are the Holy Bible (Old and New testaments). To Hindus, the scriptures include the Vedas, Upanishad, Gita and Śruti. These constitute just a few similarities and differences. They, and other comparisons mentioned in this book, are not meant to gauge which one is better but as background information.

India's spirit of culture and unity remains alive and very strong in large part due to its common religion, literature, and civilization. As Hinduism spread throughout the years, India has witnessed many historical social and political changes, most recently due to Great Britain's influence and dominance. Yet, India's spiritual unity not only remained but has been fostered and spread. Perhaps Hinduism's strength and longevity are because it does not have limitations, such as comparing itself to other religions.

In Hinduism, intellect is subordinate to intuition, dogma to experience, outward expression to inward realization and transformation. Hinduism is life itself. It rests in its devotees' faith. Unlike other religions, Hindus readily admit to other points of view and accept and respect them as such. Hindus believe that if the whole race of humanity is the creation of God, then their opinions and beliefs are worthy of respect, no matter how varied their opinions. There is a legendary story that two Hindu men worshipped different gods. One worshipped Vishnu, and the other worshiped Shiva. When they were both at a temple, the worshipper of Vishnu only bowed to Vishnu's image and not Shiva's. Then Vishnu's image suddenly divided itself in half, and Shiva appeared on one side of the image and Vishnu on the other side. The two images smiled on the disrespectful and bigoted worshipper and told him that Vishnu and Shiva were one and the same. Thus, what matters most is not converting worshippers. What matters most in Hinduism is the person's proper conduct.

The three main gods in Hinduism consists of Brahma, the creator, Vishnu, the preserver, and Shiva the destroyer who recreates. However, it is important to note that Hinduism is much broader and much more complex than having gods and deities and categorizing them. Hinduism is also human imagination. The human imagination transcends nature, the supernatural, and even the divine. In Hinduism, our human brains and imagination play a crucial part in defining our very humanity. From our imagination comes our vision of the world, our vision of the past, our vision of our future, and, most importantly, our vision of ourselves. In Hinduism, it is the imagination that makes us a part of yet distinct from nature. In short, imagination makes us self-aware. It is this ever-important self-awareness that pushes us to improve and develop as humans. In our quest for improvement lies logic. One way we have garnered logic and understanding of ourselves and the universe is through oral tradition.

One of the most ancient of Hinduism's Holy oral traditions is the Vedas, which are believed to have been first directly revealed by God to the Aryans in the second millennium B.C. and, through the years, preserved through further oral tradition. Later, the Vedas were written in Sanskrit. The Vedas consist of the Rig Veda, Sama Veda, Yajur Veda, and the Atharva Veda. The literal meaning of Veda is "understanding." There exist other Hindu Holy texts such as Ramayana, Bhagavad Gita, and the Mahabharta, which were also written in Sanskrit, a language that is nearly four thousand years old and is believed to be the dialogue of Hindu gods. I was fortunate that my guide read Sanskrit and was able to translate the language on many ancient statues we visited.

The only "training" before my sojourn to India was my World Religion class with Dr. Habito at Southern Methodist University's Perkins Seminary. I also conducted a cursory reading of the Bhagavad Gita and the book, "The Wonder That Was India" by A. L. Basham. I wanted to limit my information about India and Hinduism so that I could enter India and learn Hinduism with a clean slate, untainted by biases or varied interpretations. I also prepared by conducting a visit to the International Society for Krishna Consciousness Temple in Dallas, Texas. Here is the discourse that greatly aided me for my pilgrimage.

Preparation Interview Before My Pilgrimage

In preparation for my pilgrimage to India, I conducted an informal interview with Mr. Nityananda Chandra Das, a Hare Krishna minister at the Society for Krishna Consciousness Temple in Dallas, Texas. Per his request, we interviewed in their chapel where worshippers actively prayed and performed Japa with strings of beads (similar to Catholic rosary). Some worshippers blew conch shells, invoking the spirits. Incense pervaded the entire chapel.

Mr. Chandra began with a quote from the Bhagavad Gita: "Never was there a time when I did not exist, nor you, nor all these kings; nor in the future shall any of us cease to be."

First, I asked Mr. Chandra to define Hare Krishna. He stated that Hare Krishna is a movement that is a branch of Hinduism, formerly known as *Gaudiya Vaishnavism*. *Hare* means *supreme absolute being*. *Krishna* means black dark, the reincarnation of God Vishnu. According to Mr. Chandra, 70% of Hindus in the U.S. follow Hare Krishna practices.

I asked him to explain the basic structure of Hinduism, specifically, "What does your religion see as the human problematic?"

He responded, "The 'spiritual' problem is one that is beyond humanity. There is a misconception that we 'are' these (our) bodies. It is a *maya (illusion)*. We are the 'soul' within the body."

I followed with, "What is your religion's resolution to the human problematic (ultimate destiny)?"

He responded, "Our resolution is to become realized, that we are called to be a lover and servant of God. For example, our hand is greater than its own separate part. If we could only feed our parts (such as the hand), what would happen to the rest of our body?"

My next question: "What are Hindus' prescriptions/steps toward ultimate destiny?"

He replied, "The actual Hare Krishna, the chanting of holy mantra of god's name, is the most practical and impotent means of becoming God-conscious/achieving our spiritual development for this time in life." He added that "Each Yuga (years of change) has its own specific prescription. Each Yuga lasts about 1,000 years (a millennium), then it changes."

My other questions included: "Do you think American Hare Krishnas are seen as different from Hare Krishnas in India or any other country? If so, in what ways are they seen as different?"

He responded, "It depends on who is the seer. For the last seventy-five years (approximately), Indians have had their eyes on American Hare Krishnas with hopes of becoming similar, to become more modern."

I followed with "What do you believe is the best lesson Hinduism teaches?"

He replied, "That our identity is different from our body and our mind."

I asked if he had a favorite religious quote or text. "Yes," Mr. Chandra responded. "It is from the Bhagavad Gita, Chapter 10. Krishna says, 'To those who are devoted to serving me with pure love, I give them the knowledge by which they can come back to me.'"

I asked Mr. Chandra, "What keeps you faithful to Hindu?"

He stated, "My experience and the practical experience of

God's reciprocation."

"What do you think is the biggest misconception about Hindu?" I asked.

He responded, "It depends on the group or the audience. If they are Americans, they think this religion is a new thing when, in fact, it may be one of the oldest."

Finally, I mentioned to Mr. Chandra that I would be traveling to India that summer to learn more about all religions in India. "What is some advice you can provide me about learning religion in India?"

He stated, "You must visit Vrindavan (a holy town in Uttar Pradesh) where the Hindu deity Krishna is said to have spent his childhood. And keep an open mind. There are many religions within Hinduism. For example, in Varanasi, there will be many anti-theological people. Which is to say they don't believe in a separate God. Instead, they believe that God is an energy, the oneness of everything. But every religion encompasses three strands: The majority of Hindus practice *karma-kanda* (to improve material benefit). Also, there are Hindus who want release from suffering (Nirvana) and are not interested in material pursuit. Most rare will be the *Bhakti,* those yearning to only serve God and not go to heaven, necessary; just to love and serve God."

**A Christian in India:
Lessons from a Seminarian Who Discovers Jesus in
Hindu Temples**

"You will seek me and find me when you seek me with all your heart" (Jeremiah 29:13 AKJV)

"fides quaerens intellectum"

2

I

Arrival — New Delhi Neighborhood

"The most terrible loneliness is the feeling of being unloved" (Mother Teresa).

Day 1

One a.m., as my taxi driver passed littered neighborhoods strewed with beggars sleeping in tuk-tuks and cardboard on the sidewalks next to cows and buffalo, I began to pray that he was lost. He appeared lost, looking back and forth at scribbling on a paper with directions that a friendly Indian man wrote down for me at the Indira Gandhi International Airport. I prayed and prayed that my taxi driver was lost. I thought, "My hotel cannot possibly be in these horrible neighborhoods."

My taxi driver turned a corner; the neighborhood became a bit better, but not by much. Now, mostly stray dogs littered the streets. I had never witnessed so many stray dogs in one block. I counted eighteen of them. Street vendors stoked fires in pits, in which they cooked their food, and shooed the stray dogs away.

On the next corner were more streetlights and a movie theatre. My hotel stood at the end of this block. I had to walk one block; as I walked on the littered street, I noticed cow dung everywhere; the horrible pungent smell of raw sewage permeated the streets. Never had I smelled anything so bad. The Prime Balaji Deluxe Hotel on 8574 Arakashan Road, Paharganj, and New Delhi awaited my arrival.

As soon as I entered my hotel room at the Prime Balaji Deluxe Hotel, I took a cold shower. I was dirty after a nine-hour flight from Amsterdam (and a connecting twelve-hour flight from Chicago). I 'felt' even dirtier after walking down this block.

After my shower, I hopped on my clean bed. I said to myself, "I'm not leaving my hotel." Then I got up and looked out the huge window. As I looked out the window, I asked, "My God, what in the world did I get myself into by coming to India?" The smell, the poverty. "I'm never coming out of my hotel room." I thought. I could not erase the many negative images that abounded of poor, almost naked, people, including children, sleeping on dirty sidewalks in the sweltering heat. After a good sleep, I awoke and drank a hot cup of Kapi (coffee). I returned to sleep for another five hours.

"I laid me down and slept; I awakened; for the Lord sustained me" (Psalm 3:5 AKJV).

When I awoke, I felt great. I thought, "I'll check out the neighborhood." I had in mind to venture out a bit but stay close to my hotel; I had no particular sights in mind to visit until the next day, as I had already made arrangements with the hotel's tourist office. I was on my way to self-discovery.

II

Exploring the Neighborhood

"He who sees all beings in his Self and his Self in all beings, never suffers because then he sees all creatures within his true self, then jealousy, grief and hatred vanish" (The Upanishads).

Day 2

Today was 109 degrees Fahrenheit (42.7 degrees Celsius). I ventured outside about 3 p.m. Thousands of people dodged each other as they briskly walked to and fro. Cars, tuk-tuks, and commercial trucks were bottle-necked and gridlocked in traffic jams. The temperature was very similar to Texas. So, I felt fine. As I walked, I marveled at all the paintings, billboards, posters, and statues of the many gods, goddesses, and swamis who were praised, lauded, and eulogized by their community and followers. I thought, "Christian territory does not exist here." In my previous travels to Rome, Venice, and Paris, I took for granted Christianity's effect on those communities.

The aroma coming from the street vendors who cooked food on open fires was exotic and delicious. Spicy smells to my American sense of smells, but not unusual to my Mexican heritage's rich cuisine. Also catching my attention were the immense bright and

New Delhi Neighborhood

beautifully brilliant colors that decorated the streets of New Delhi. Just about every object for sale along the sidewalks, including fruits, vegetables and spices, shined: dazzling greens which symbolize new beginnings, harvest, fertility; glaring reds which symbolize purity and sensuality; saffron, the most sacred color of Hindus; vibrant yellows, the color of knowledge, and intense blues which symbolize water and sky.

    Returning to the Prime Balaji Deluxe Hotel, I walked on broken and trash-littered sidewalks contrasting with the illuminated and beautiful hues of the environment. To my right, I suddenly noticed a half-naked, older, dark Indian man (wearing only a loincloth) literally rolling on the hot asphalt street. As the man tumbled on the hot street, he landed halfway under a parked commercial truck. I stopped and stared at this sight; I wondered if he was OK. Was I to offer him any help? Did he need water? However, I soon noticed that other people just jumped over him and minded their own business; pedestrians just kept walking, dodging, springing, darting—nothing unusual here, it seemed. Was he a Dalit, a person from the untouchable caste? Was he a mendicant (monk) or sadhu (priest) who has renounced the worldly life? I could not tell, as I could not see his face; most sadhus adopt the appearance of Shiva by painting their faces and allowing their hair to grow long and worn in a knot or bun on top of their heads. Regardless of who this man was, I felt sad for him and helpless. He seemed as though he was in some kind of trance, his eyes tightly closed. I did not know what to do or whether I was even "allowed" to do anything, so I did nothing. I was in another world, after all. I could only make a mental note to pray for him upon my return to my hotel.

Indian Mendicant

8

As I walked the crowded and lively neighborhood, I recalled that I had previously seen a man cutting hair by a sidewalk stand, so I searched for him. About three blocks later, I found him and his assistant. I stopped at his haircut stand and pointed to my hair. I obviously needed a haircut. He sat me down and sprayed my hair with a dirty water bottle. He combed it with a filthy black comb. I didn't care because I needed a haircut. As I took in the neighborhood, I observed that many Indian men seemed to have good haircuts, so I wanted to fit in. As I was getting my haircut, I noticed that there were mostly men walking about. Some were holding hands (a custom in India). But women were, for the most part, absent. I believed the ratio to be fifty to one.

The barber asked me something In Hindi. But I didn't understand. So, I just nodded, "Yes." He began to perform karate chops on my head. I guess I had consented to a head massage of sorts. As my head violently jolted, popped, and twisted, I wished I spoke Hindi. I would have told him, "No, thanks." As I paid the hairdresser (Indian rupees proved easy to understand), he and his assistant swayed their head from left to right. I understood this represented a sign of endearment.

Approximately two blocks from the haircut stand stood a food vendor (one of hundreds); when the man asked for my order, I simply pointed to whatever a customer next to me was eating. I noticed he spoke to me in Hindi. Due to my dark skin, I assumed he thought I was Indian. The vendor gestured for me to have a seat at a dirty wooden table near the busy street. I sat and wondered if tuk-tuks or cars would hit my table as they quickly zipped by inches away from it. As I waited for my food, I enjoyed the immense commotion and noisy tumult which accompanied the heavy traffic and everyday pandemonium that comes with 21 million inhabitants.

When my plate of food arrived, it was absent any utensils, only a brown chapatti, flatbread; I quickly realized the chapatti would be my utensil. This reminded me of my upbringing of eating everything with Mexican tortillas. So, I felt like a natural. The dish consisted of a very small serving of lentils called dal makhani; it was very delicious and extremely spicy. I recognized the smell and taste of cumin, ginger, ajwain, and cardamom spices. After lunch, I headed back to my hotel and slept for the rest of the day. I still felt jetlagged, fatigued, malaise, and lacked concentration, but at least I was now full.

"Better is a dinner of herbs where love is, than a stalled ox and hatred therewith" (Proverbs 15:17 AKJV).

III

The Taj Mahal

"Did you ever build a castle in the air? Here is one, brought down to earth and fixed for the wonder of ages." (Bayard Taylor).

Day 3

Seven a.m. Awoken by the alarm, I quickly dressed. My hotel tour guide awaited me in the hotel lobby. Today, I planned to see the famous Taj Mahal, a three-hour drive south from New Delhi. My 29-year-old Indian tour guide greeted me warmly; he seemed rather tall for your 'average' Indian male.

I sat in the front of his air-conditioned car per his request. We made the usual small talk (Where are you from? Where do I work? Marital status, etc.) I mentioned that my stay consisted of learning the Hindu religion and seeing mostly Hindu temples.

As we drove, I measured my guide's driving as either the worst I had ever witnessed or the best, depending on one's perspective. He parried, negotiated, and even manipulated the roads like a master Indy 500 winner. I noticed on the speedometer that he was driving 90 miles per hour (approx. 150 km/h).

Halfway to Agra, we stopped at a convenience store/restaurant. Thank goodness the menus had pictures. I asked my

English-speaking guide, "Which are the breakfast plates?" He suggested a breakfast plate that was very spicy, yet delicious. We stood at a table and ate our delicious breakfast of dosas (thin crepes) and idlis (spiced potatoes). During breakfast, I mentioned to my guide that I walked around my hotel's neighborhood the previous day. I added that I noticed that there were very few females in and around the neighborhood. He casually explained that women have no business around the town; he added, "they are at home, taking care of home responsibilities."

After our delicious breakfast, my sojourn to Agra continued; my guide explained that there would be another guide in Agra who would meet me there and give me the Taj Mahal tour. This was not told to me earlier at the hotel when I originally made my plans, and this news made me uneasy. How could I meet a perfect stranger three hours from my hotel who may or may not be known by the hotel owners?

My guide's surprise news reminded me of the movies where the main character meets a perfect stranger holding a mysterious black briefcase and wearing a London Fog coat.

My uneasiness worsened. As we drove at breakneck speeds on the highway, where men pulled over to urinate in public view without thinking twice, my driver/travel guide nonchalantly asked me, "Do you want to buy marijuana?" Although he spoke broken English, I understood exactly what he asked.

Not wanting to appear unnerved, I casually responded, "No, I'm good." Then a few miles later, I asked him, "Why would you ask me that question?"

He responded, "'Because you are American. And a lot of American tourists ask me to buy marijuana for them."

I said, "Oh. I see." He went on to explain that I must be careful because people in India will ask tourists to buy marijuana then quickly report them to the local police. The tourists, in turn, have to pay the police to get out of trouble. He then said the famous last words, "But you can trust me." And "I have all the time marijuana." Then, he proudly pointed and patted his left front blue jean pocket.

I was angry at his offer. As I sat on the passenger side of the taxi, I stared out the car window. I thought *Great. Now I'm traveling with a drug dealer. Here I am in a foreign country, miles away from my hotel and thousands of miles from my home, and I am traveling with a drug dealer. Furthermore, I am soon to meet yet another perfect stranger in Agra. Fantastic!* To comfort myself, I silently prayed, "Ye shall not fear them: for the Lord your God he shall fight for you" (Deuteronomy 3:22 AKJV). I began to calm down.

Finally, in Agra. I met my new guide. He was a pleasant man who talked very quickly and did not allow me to ask questions. Perhaps he had another tourist waiting on him after me, I thought. He did a wonderful job showing me around the magnificent and

The Taj Mahal

majestic Taj Mahal that manifested itself a grand sight. The graceful and exquisite beauty of the ivory-white marble mausoleum situated on the south bank of the Yamuna River had always been on my "to visit" list. The history: the love story of Shah Jahan (reigned from 1628-1658) and his favorite wife Mumtaz will stand as one of the most beautiful love stories in human history. The mosque and guest house next to it added an extra surprise that I hadn't expected and had never even heard of. The Taj Majal's arresting opulence and estimated costs immensely challenged my imagination because I was in a country where approximately 25 percent live in poverty. The immensely majestic building seemed and felt as I would imagine a palace in God's Heaven would be.

> *"For every house is built by someone, but God is the builder of everything" (Hebrews 3:4 AKJV).*

IV

Birla Temple

"Your duty is to treat everybody with love as a manifestation of the Lord" (Swami Sivananda).

Day 4

While enjoying my delectable Indian breakfast (dosas, crepes made of lentils, idles, steamed rice pancakes and spiced potatoes) at the Balaji Deluxe Hotel, I met an American woman from New York. She had been in India a week already. We began to make small talk, and she gave me the phone number of a tour guy with whom she had recently had a wonderful experience. After my horrible experience with my young guide the day before, I did not want to be exposed to any danger again. I immediately called my new friend's guide, and (thank God) he accommodated my tour plans that same day. His name was Mr. Harsh Rana, a 50-something-year-old married father of one child; he would be my new tour guide (except for one remaining day with my previous tour guide which I had paid for in advance. I wondered what surprises awaited me then).

Today's high was forecasted to be 110 degrees Fahrenheit (43 degrees Celsius). The first visit for my new guide and I was The Holy Birla Mandir Temple in Jaipur (also known as Laxmi Narayan).

The Birla Temple

The temple's name refers to two different Hindu temples in one location that were built by the Birla family. The Birla Temple was merely two miles from my hotel.

The two Holy Mandirs stand as a dedication to Laxmi, the beautiful Goddess of prosperity, and Narayana, the preserver. Mahatma Gandhi, the famous Indian activist, inaugurated this beautiful temple on the condition that people of all castes would be allowed to enter it.

Flowers for sale for offerings to Hindu gods (Pooja Ritual)

As we entered the Birla Temple, we stopped at a stand outside the temple's gate to buy garlands of beautiful flowers (jasmines, red hibiscus, marigolds, and palash, to name a few). We took off our shoes and placed them in a small closet area. As we entered, I noticed Mr. Rana touched the entrance steps with his right hand, and then, with the same hand, he touched his heart. He would repeat this ritual at every temple henceforth. I followed suit. Within the Birla's beautiful temples, many other gods were situated inside small altars decorated with bright colors and flowers while incense burned, creating a mystical aura. In some altars, men sat and received our offerings of flowers; one attendant gave our offering to the respective gods and returned them to us. Then, he gave us two spoons full of holy water; one to wet your head and the other to drink. I merely followed my guide's gestures and actions. These offerings are similar to the second part of a Catholic Mass, which focuses on offerings: the monetary collection offering, the offering of the bread and wine to be consecrated, and the Eucharist itself.

The most impactful and significant feeling I received at the Birla Temple was the immense spirituous feeling of unity of the holy spirits or gods which resided in these temples. Their unity felt as if they represented one loving, united, and welcoming family. I wished more people could experience this wonderful and unique feeling. I thought that if this wonderful experience was a representation of what I would further experience In India, I was in for a wonderful treat and would not be disappointed. Although I did not know at the time, this Hindu temple would serve as a foreshadow for the rest of my stay in beautiful India.

At that temple, I was also reminded of Jesus Christ. I believed these gods also existed for one purpose: to protect and love humans. Not only did the temples' historic significance touch my heart, but they also helped me understand their inspirational, meaningful, and significant reasons for their existence. I was reminded of Hebrews 2:17 AKJV: "Wherefore in all things it behoved him to be made like unto his brethren, that he might be a merciful and faithful high priest in things pertaining to God."

During meditative reflection, I thought of our offerings of beautiful flowers and the act of dousing our head with holy water and drinking it. The offerings to the Hindu gods made me feel that these acts not only represented a physical demonstrative act, but a responsive and meaningful expression of my gratitude of the Hindu gods' love and care for me, a foreigner with a different religious belief.

Next to the magnificent Birla Temple stood a Buddhist temple. There was no official name for it. At first, I found it odd that a Buddhist temple stood next to a Hindu temple on the same property. I had understood these two religions as mutually exclusive. It would be akin to having a Baptist church on the same property as a Catholic church. But to Hindus, Buddhism is an extension of and coexistence with Hinduism.

Siddhartha Gautama founded Buddhism sometime in the 6th or 5th century B.C.E. Inside this small temple sat a dazzling golden statue of a heavy-set Buddha. The notion that penury was literally around the corner from this golden statue addled my thinking. Although Buddhism and Hinduism both agree on karma, dharma, moksha and reincarnation, Buddhism rejects Hinduism's formal rituals and its caste system. Buddhism strongly urges its followers to seek enlightenment through meditation.

This small temple was protected by a small gate and a small lock. I could not understand how they expected that such a small lock would secure a golden statue. I asked Mr. Rana, "Is this all the security the Buddha has?" as I touched the lock. He responded,

"Who would dare steal it?"

Like the many posters, billboards, statues of gods, goddesses and swami pictures, posters, statues and paintings that adorned the roads and buildings, my guide's response to the small lock reminded me of a famous American saying: "I am not in Kansas anymore." Did I hold the key to understanding these gods or, at a minimum, understand their purpose(s)?

The Buddha's security lock evoked in me a verse from Matthew:

> *"And I will give unto thee the keys of the kingdom of heaven: and whatsoever thou shalt bind on earth shall be bound in heaven: and whatsoever thou shalt loose on earth shall be loosed in heaven" (Matthew 16:19 AKJV).*

V

Gurudwara Bangla Sahib Temple, Lotus Temple

"It is divinity that shapes not only your acts, but also your words and thoughts." (Swami Sivananda)

Day 5: Holy Gurudwara Bangla Sahib Temple

One of the most prominent Sikh temples (located in Connaught

Gurudwara Bangla Sahib Sikh Temple

Place and first built in 1664), the Holy Gurdwara Bangla Sahib Temple represents "the gateway to the Guru." Known for its association with the eighth Sikh Guru, Har Krishna, the gurdwara stands gracefully adorned with gold leaf domes and an outside pool, a "sarovar." The temple's stunning grand entrance illuminated our approach with bright metallic multi-colors. Before we entered, we needed to cover our heads with turbans, which there were plenty to choose from of various bright and beautiful hews. From outside the temple, we heard live music playing inside. This devotional and communal singing known as "Kirtan" originated from the holy book. Songs can be either scripture or legends.

Before entering, in addition to covering our heads, we needed to wash our feet. We also purchased aromatic garlands of jasmine, red hibiscus, marigolds, and palash flowers for our offerings.

After taking a tour inside this beautiful Sikh temple and making our offerings to the gutka, the holy book, we sat and listened to the enchanting Kirtan music, which embodies and magnifies the emotional appeal of the lyrics. Typical instruments include the tabla, harmonium, karatala, and stringed instruments. Prayers are also recited to music as a way of remembering and understanding the sanctified words in the holy book. Like Catholic Litany prayers, many prayers in this temple involved antiphonary, wherein one person says a part of the prayer and the rest of the congregation follows with unified responses.

Soon after, we walked to a large adjacent building similar to a gymnasium. There we sat on a large carpet on the concrete floor with approximately 100 other people and held in front of us a tin plate which we had picked up at the entrance. A large man walked around holding a huge pot and deposited hot lentils on our tin plates. The servers kept returning to ask if we wanted more lentils every five minutes.

The offerings, covering one's head, and washing one's feet before entering not only demonstrated respect but also signified the people's submission to the words and the spirit of the sanctified holy book. Money donated to the temple helped pay for the food offered daily to all welcomed visitors, the homeless, and the sick. Their daily humanitarian effort to feed the hungry and homeless was most admirable, indeed. While we sat on a long rug placed on the concrete floor and ate, I could not finish my lentils. So, my guide, Mr. Rana, finished them for me. He said it would be disrespectful not to finish the food.

The temple's architecture included khandas and chakkars. The khanda is a double-edged sword that represents the belief in one God. The chakkar, like the kara, is circular, denoting God without beginning and end. This was similar to my Christian God's words, "I am the Alpha and the Omega" (Revelation 22:13 AKJV).

I discerned a very powerful and loving welcome in this Sikh temple as if being welcomed by a family that provided water (to drink and wash), cleansing (for my feet), food, and clothing (a turban). I perceived the people's profound respect for their venerated book was unlimited and boundless. Their holy book also possessed a large decorative bed (sukhasan) where it rests at night. In addition to Hinduism, the Sikh religion is one of the oldest religions (believed to have begun around 1500 CE.)

After departing the Holy Gurdwara, a consecrated place with venerable customs and traditions similar to my Christian Church, a biblical verse from Jesus resonated: "For I was an hungred, and ye gave me meat: I was thirsty, and ye gave me drink" (Matthew 25:35-40 AKJV).

The Bahai Lotus Temple

Our next temple: The Bahai Lotus Temple. Constructed of

The Lotus Temple

white marble and taking the shape of a lotus flower, the Lotus Temple sits among beautiful lush green gardens. Nine pools of water accompany its beautiful structure. To Hindus, the white lotus flower represents beauty and purity. The God Brahma is believed to have been born from a lotus flower. The unfolding of the lotus flower's leaves speaks to the expansion of one's soul and one's spiritual awakening. Lotus flowers have appeared in Hindu, Buddhist, Jain, and Islamic texts for many years. Considered a salient temple, the Lotus is a "silent/quiet temple" which allows only silence once one is inside its structure. Only seven of these temples exist in the world, albeit in varied designs. The others are in North America, Panama, Germany, Uganda, Australia, and Samoa. But none are in the design of a lotus flower except the one in India.

As I quietly sat with a group of approximately twenty people from all over the world inside the Lotus Temple's white marbled grandeur, I contemplated our coalesced silence. Our silence created energy and power, a concentration of contemplation. Our coalesced silence stood as a grand gesture of respect to the Holy

Spirit that was felt everywhere. Our consolidated silence mutually acknowledged God's glory.

After exiting this temple, I recalled that before our group entered the Lotus Temple, a young Indian tour guide stated to our group, "Welcome all to this place of peace and blessings for all religions." "Faultless" would describe the young guide's foreboding words. Although our group only consisted of about sixty tourists made up of all nationalities, our presence and our mutual silence represented the entire world's prayer of peace. The spiritual power of silence is greatly underrated; its power to reflect, create, and discover provides an opportunity not only to connect with our own souls but also to the souls of others and, ultimately, to our unified actions.

> *"[There is] a time to keep silence, and a time to speak" (Ecclesiastes 3:7 AKJV).*

VI

ISKCON Temple, Swaminarayan Akshardham Temple

"The spiritual knowledge of the soul, of God and transcendental knowledge is both purifying a liberating" (Bhagavad Gita).

Day 6: Sri Sri Radha Parthasarathi Mandir (also known as ISKCON, International Society for Krishna Consciousness).

In this Holy Temple, Lord Krishna is its main God. Worshipped as the eighth avatar of the god Vishnu and a God in his own right, a God of compassion, tenderness and love, Lord Krishna portrays many stages and perspectives in his life; Lord Krishna may appear as an infant, a music lover, a ladies' lover, a charioteer, and a dancer.

My tour guide, Mr. Rana, had never visited this temple. As heat exhaustion dictated our pace (it was about 3 p.m., the sun at its peak at 110 degrees Fahrenheit (43 degrees Celsius)), we slowly walked a bit slower up the Hare Krishna Hill, east of Kailas. We sauntered confused and somewhat lost because we could not find the main entrance to this huge temple. Upon finally finding the main entrance of this immense temple, I immediately

ISKCON Temple

noticed a statute of Abhay Charanaravinda Bhaktivedanta Swami Prabhupāda. I recognized him immediately since I had previously visited an ISKCON temple in Dallas, Texas as part of an assignment for my World Religion Class. Abhay Charanaravinda Bhaktivedanta Swami Prabhupāda was an Indian Hindu spiritual teacher and the founder preceptor of the International Society for Krishna Consciousness (ISKCON), commonly known as the "Hare Krishna Movement;" he was born in 1896 in Kolkata, India.

Extreme liveliness would be my description of this temple. A group of worshipers sang, danced, and played instruments in the middle of the temple. In blissful ecstasy and trancelike state, the worshippers happily sang and walked around the temple as other worshipers joined them and happily partook in the festive singing and dancing. Some worshipers rolled on the floor as well, while others crawled.

Even though we arrived at this temple tired and fatigued, the

A.C. Bhaktivedanta Swami Prabhupāda

wonderful festive aura and merry atmosphere greatly invigorated our spirits. I came out of this temple feeling carefree, energized, delighted, and joyous at life. The following verse reverberated in my thoughts:

"Thou hast turned for me my mourning into dancing: thou hast put off my sackcloth, and girded me with gladness; to the end that my glory may sing praise to thee, and not be silent. O Lord my

Swaminarayan Akshardham Temple

God, I will give thanks unto thee forever" (Psalm 30:11-12 AKJV).

The final temple we visited on this day was Swaminarayan Akshardham Temple. Swaminarayan is the primary deity of this temple. Born in Chhapaiya, India, in 1781, Swaminarayan was a yogi whose life teachings brought a revival of Hindu practices. He is believed by his devotees to be the manifestation of God. Other idols in this temple included Shiv Parvati, Sita Ram, Lakshmi Narayana, and Rhada Krishna. The temple's size and beauty will leave any visitor awestruck. Its immense size radiates not only beauty but peace, divinity, and grandeur. Its structure stands as a very unique temple because its design originated from another swami, Pramukh Swami Maharaj.

Some of this temple's stunning and alluring external marble walls stood 611 feet long and five feet tall. They included 200 sculptured figures of various Hindu gods and goddesses. The temple's splendid garden displayed grand water fountains. It also consisted of ten gates. In one gate alone, there were 208 sculptured dual forms of gods and their devotees. Included on the grounds: the white marbled footprints of Bhagwan Swaminarayan which remind its visitors of his reincarnation on earth. These footprints also contain the 16 sacred signs of God (the bottom of each foot represent various beliefs), similar to reading one's palms.

The temple's immense beauty from a distance can only be surpassed by its gold and priceless jewels which adorn the center where Lord Swaminarayan sits. Never have I witnessed such opulence and homage paid with such splendor. While I understood its symbolic magnificence, the practicality of grasping (let alone understanding) such luxury and lavishness left me dumbfounded. Its magnificence and grandeur exemplified an inner spirit's abundance of celestial enlightenment.

> *"For, behold, I create new heavens and a new earth: and the former shall not be remembered, nor come into mind" (Isaiah 65:17 AKJV).*

Garden of Swaminarayan Akshardham Temple

VII

Tera Manzil, The Himalayas, Haridwar: The Holy Ganges

"When you are searching and seeking, you should be doing it honestly with your full strength—not halfheartedly" (Swami Rama).

Day 7: Tera Manzil Temple, Rishikesh

Located in Uttarakhand, northeast India, a four-hour drive from New Delhi, Rishikesh sits along the Himalayan foothills beside the Ganges River. It is also considered the center of studying yoga. Tera Manzil Temple is shaped like a multi-layered cake; this thirteen-level pink temple houses at least eight mini-rooms (altars) of worship on each floor. Unlike other temples that are dedicated to a single deity, Tera Manzil houses multiple deities and offers an opportunity to worship all of them in a single locale. Located on the banks of the Holy Ganges River and next to the beginning of the Himalaya Mountains, the abode of gods, this background provides an amazing panoramic scene from any level of the Tera Manzil Temple.

The Himalaya mountain range stretches to Pakistan and Tibet, through Bhutan, and ends in Myanmar. They include

The Himalaya Mountains

over fifty mountains, which stand 7,200 meters in elevation. Of these mountains, the highest is Mount Everest. Meru is another mountain; its peak is 21,000 feet (6400.8 meters). Meru is the seat of the gods; the Lotus mountain represents the inner-most part of people's hearts. Many Hindus believe that everyone holds a holy mountain in their hearts. Yes, there are also ancient temples atop these mystical mountains.

These Himalaya mountains collectively have been personified as Himavat, who was the ruler of the Himalaya kingdom and father of Goddess Parvati and the Goddess Ganga of ancient India.

Many Hindus consider the Himalayas a microcosm of life itself and the abode of the gods. The mountain range climates vary from tropical weather at the foot of the mountains, to an environment of clay and marsh, to desolate ice caps. However varied, every environment provides sustenance for its inhabitants. The Himalayas not only have an important role in influencing the climate in India, but they are also considered an epicenter of spirituality for many Hindu visitors; they find spiritual guidance and divine inspiration on these majestic mountains. Because of their holiness, many peaks of the Himalayas' mountains are off-limits to climbers. Black river stones by the banks of the beginning of the River Ganga are considered to have special powers and are much sought after and used in altars. In fact, they can stand as their own altar.

The Tera Manzil Temple stands, in many ways, as an extension of the Himalayas' spirit. Although I was unsure whether I could physically climb all the stairs to the top thirteenth floor, I gave it a try, nonetheless. On my way up, my guide, Mr. Rana, stopped at the shrine of his favorite Goddess, Kali. She is the reincarnation of the Parvati, wife of Shiva. Kali wears a necklace made of severed heads and a skirt made of severed arms. Her tongue and her sword drip with blood. Kali means "she who is black." She represents the goddess of the apocalypse, death, and time. She embodies power and tough love. Her approach is harsh but her inner purpose is good. What she does is not out of evil. Instead, it is out of compassion. Her compassion awakens you so that you can grow and face your demons—whether you are ready or not. She intends to break you out of your shell so that you can see your own inner

Tera Manzil Temple

strength to help you achieve your goals. Kali will throw you into hardships so that you can learn on your own, the hard way. She takes this approach for people who want a quick solution to their problems (physical, mental, or spiritual). She cuts to the chase and puts you on the 'fast track' to achieving your goals. Her mantra is "Salutations. I bring to me she who is dark and powerful."

When we finally reached the top tier of the Tera Manzil Temple (about 25 minutes total), the Hindu priest (known as pujari) received my offering and applied a tilaka on my forehead; he looked deep into my eyes and asked, "Where are you from?" I had not even opened my mouth. How did he know I was a foreigner?

The tilaka, made of orange-colored sandalwood paste, was applied to the space between my eyebrows; this spot on our forehead is believed to be the place of intuition and is said to take the individual's thoughts towards spirituality, which is an important purpose of any religious act.

On the 13th floor, I took a moment to take in this beautifully amazing sight of the natural, the Himalayas, and the holy, the Ganges. I was reminded of the holy Christian day of Ash Wednesday (the first day of Lent) when Christians bear the sign of the cross on their forehead, a practice that is thousands of years old. This was the first tilaka I had received in India; therefore, it represented something very special to me.

As I took a few moments to meditate and take in the majestic panorama that I beheld, a powerful feeling overcame my thoughts. "For the invisible things of him from the creation of the world are clearly seen" (Romans 1:20 AKJV).

After the Tera Manzil Temple, we drove to Haridwar, Uttarakhand, about 20 minutes away. Haridwar is famous for its Ganga Aarti, worship of the river Ganges where Hindu ceremonies are held nightly at Har-ki-Pauri ghat. Haridwar is also the place

Mother Ganga (The Ganges River)

where all pilgrims' names and their family names are preserved for all time. Mr. Rana mentioned that his name and his family names were in that book dating four generations.

Personalized as the Goddess Ganga, this lively and engaging river's water embodies sacredness and is primarily considered the most sacred water for every Hindu; it is believed that the river was a gift from Shiva to a king who had led a saintly life so that he could clean the souls of his ancestors. The river was originally in heaven, but when it was transferred to earth for the king, it crashed so hard that it threatened to drown many people and destroy many cities. To calm its effects, Shiva tamed the river's power with his long thick hair. To date, the holy Ganges River flows calmly from the Himalaya mountains to the south of India.

Mother Ganga is also referred to as the river with three heads because it is believed that she flows in Heaven, Earth, and the underworld. The rituals in Mother Ganga, as it is locally known, abound, such as bathing in her holy water, which causes the remission of one's sins and facilitates Moksha, the liberation from the cycle of life and death. The Holy Ganga represents the direct and sacred medium of connecting with the divine power.

Many Hindus make a pilgrimage from one end of the river to the other. This pilgrimage is considered the ultimate spiritual pilgrimage. The length of Mother Ganga is 1,569 miles (2525.061 kilometers). This pilgrimage requires daily bathing in the Ganga and fasting throughout the duration of one's pilgrimage. However, what is most important about a pilgrimage is not the physical travel, but the inner pilgrimage, i.e., one's inner transformation.

Also, many Hindus go to the city of Varanasi to die. Varanasi is approximately a thirteen-hour drive south of New Delhi. Mother Ganga passes through this ancient city and welcomes the sick and the dying. There are over two thousand temples in Varanasi alone. Once Hindus die in Varanasi, their bodies are cremated and their ashes put in the river as their last request. Hindu cremation is done in the open and considered one of the rites of passage. At the time of cremation, last rites, also known as Pujas prayers, are recited. When Hindus' ashes are put in the river, it is believed that the souls of the departed merge with the souls of their ancestors.

All Hindus must be cremated except holy priests, because Hindus believe they have no sins. Their bodies are wrapped in a shroud, weighted, and put in the river without cremation. Hindus last rites are similar to those in Catholicism, which are performed toward the end of one's life and include confession, Holy Communion, and anointment. To Hindus, Varanasi symbolizes the whole world. They believe this city was the location where the world was created. All eight points of the compass congregate in Varanasi; all of time is present in Varanasi. This belief is represented in the mandala, which is used as a ritualistic and spiritual symbol in Hinduism that represents the universe.

This night, approximately two thousand Hindus congregated on both banks of the Ganga; they, like us, were here to partake in the Ganga Aarti, worship of the river Ganges ceremony. In this sacred Hindu ceremony, thousands of people purify themselves in the cold and clear water of the Holy Ganga River. If you can get close enough to the pujari or archaka (the Hindu priest) conducting the ceremony with fire offerings, you can also purify yourself with fire, smoke and heat that is offered to the Holy Ganga.

Tonight, Hindus dipped their toes, waded waist-deep, or completely submerged themselves in Mother Ganga. I also partook in the Holy Ganga's water blessing by wading waist-deep and wetting my head. I also lit a candle with flowers (known as a *diya*) and placed it on the river as I prayed along with a pujari, and I mentioned my family members by name as the pujari prompted me. I watched the flowered candle quickly flow down with Mother Ganga's strong and fast current. I had always wanted to partake in this beautiful and sacred ritual.

> *"For thou wilt light my candle: the Lord my God will enlighten my darkness" (Psalm 18:28 AKJV).*

When the Aarti ceremony was to begin, I smelled a burning scent in the night's air and noticed gray ashes floating in the sky. Mr. Rana asked me, "Do you know what that is?" I said no. He stated, "Those are ashes from a cremation that is being performed over there." He pointed to a ghat across the river. He explained that later, the priest performing tonight's ceremony would place the ashes in the Ganges. We gathered as close as we could to the main stage (which stood directly across the Ganges from our location); there the Pujari would soon be performing the Aarti. By this time, crowds quickly grew increasingly larger. This beautiful ceremony began with loud prayers followed by the crowds loudly chanting mantras, touching their heart and head repeatedly while singing. These gestures greatly reminded me of Catholics' genuflection, wherein certain prayers call for the devotee to touch the ground with their right knee, followed by making the sign of the cross on the hearts and forehead.

The sacred ritual then continued with fire illuminating from lamps which are soaked with wicks; the wicks are purified in butter or camphor; the lighted lamps were repeatedly swayed counterclockwise facing Mother Ganga, accompanied by songs in holy praise. The goal is that the lamps' fire acquire the power of the Ganga deity. Devotees cup their hands over the flame and raise their palms to their forehead to receive the Goddesses' purification and blessing. This beautiful ritual continued for approximately 90 minutes. I silently listened to the hypnotizing chants.

My guide had asked me if he could bring his teenage son to Haridwar with us, as he was still on school summer vacation. I did not see a problem with that at all. Harsh Rana was his name; he was 15 years old. At the bank of the Ganga, I asked Harsh if he practiced Hinduism. He said yes but did not too much. Yet, I noticed that as the thousands of people joined in the chants, raising their hands, and clapping, Harsh did not skip a beat. The actions of this non-practicing Hindu spoke greatly of the immensity of Hindu influence and the interwoven power on its culture and intricate interconnection within its society.

As the immense crowd continued chanting in great unison, I noticed myself staring at the beautiful glistening river as it reflected the light from the lamps and the hundreds of floating candles. Like all rivers, seas and oceans, this powerful river also represented the endless cycle of life. But unlike any river, Mother Ganga felt alive and breathing.

Enchanted by the glistening, living water, I was reminded of scripture: "He that believeth on me, as the scripture hath said out of his belly shall flow rivers of living water" (John 7:38 KJV) and "When thou passest through the waters, I will be with thee; and through the rivers, they shall not overflow thee" (Isaiah 43:2 AKJV).

A cathartic moment, this specific experience had the most impact on me of my entire trip. Similar to the spirit of God bestowed onto Jesus in the river Jordan, was the spirit of my Jesus revealing itself to me through the Ganges, the people, the love I was feeling?

I continued to permit my mind and soul to take in everything that I witnessed. I stared at the darkness of space and wondered about its infinity. And before me existed light and life. At that moment, I began to recognize and question whether considering Hindu as a separate religion and where my God fit in the schema of Hindu was even important; it was blatantly obvious. I began to release my concern about where my God fit in the Hindu schema. For the Goddess Ganga was flowing me closer to my Jesus. For this living river inundated me with my living God as I understand Him to be. And that 'perfection' was good enough for me. I continued acquiring insurmountable respect for the Hindu religion. My spiritual course and goal for my visit to India continued to develop and garner spiritual growth and divine enlightenment. How can one not feel this at this very spot, I wondered? For the fire's light which harkened the Holy Ganga spirit harkened me as well. I whispered to myself, "Jesus said, 'I am the light of the world'" (John 8:12 AKJV).

Arriving at my hotel at one a.m., I quickly fell fast asleep. I had a very vivid dream. My father and I had once visited Espada Park on the south side of my hometown of San Antonio, Texas. I had taken him out on a day pass from the nursing home where his dementia had taken him. In this dream, as in reality, I parked by a small yet fast-moving waterfall. I asked my father in Spanish, "¿Qué bonito es este parque con su aqua que nunca para de corer?" To which he replied, "Donde vivo yo, en mi pueblo tiene parques más bonitos." (Translation) "Isn't this a beautiful park dad? The water never stops running." He replied, "Where I live, my town has more beautiful parks than this." He was from Candela, Coahuila, Mexico. Then next to my dad appeared Jesus. And He said, "In my Father's house are many mansions." I awoke and washed my face with cold water. I remembered that two weeks after my dad and I visited this park in real life, he passed away from liver cancer a year to the date he was diagnosed. The direct experience was that I had my dad, my Father, and the Holy Spirit with me in India. I looked outside my hotel window into the darkness; a deluge was engulfing the entire neighborhood. The monsoon season was beginning. The monsoon season is very important as it affects the climate of India. As just as soon as it had begun, the heavy rain stopped. Like the monsoon, no longer would my pathetic fallacy intensify my inner storm.

VIII

Mathura

Sri Krishna Temple; Chhatarpur Temple, Hanuman Temple, Monkey Temple, Elephant Sanctuary, Jama Mosque, Pagal Baba Temple

"Blessed is human birth, even the dwellers in heaven desire his birth" (Krishna Janmashtami).

Day 8: Sri Krishna Janna Bhoomi Temple

At eight a.m., I had finished my breakfast in the Balaji Deluxe Hotel; it consisted of roti (flatbread) and spicy idles (rice pancakes) and coffee. Mr. Rana awaited me in the hotel lobby. Today we would begin my adventures in Mathura, a sacred city about a three-hour drive from New Delhi. It is located in Uttar Pradesh, northern India. Lord Krishna is said to have been born in this city. It is also home to the Vishram Ghat along the banks of the river Yamuna, where Lord Krishna is believed to have rested after killing Kansa, a tyrant ruler of Mathura.

After breakfast, I descended the hotel's stairs to meet my guide in the lobby. Mr. Rana saw me and quickly said, "No shorts." I had forgotten that he had previously told me that the birthplace temple of Krishna did not allow shorts, cameras or any bags. I quickly changed. The forecast predicted 110 degrees Fahrenheit (43 degrees Celsius).

As we were arriving in Mathura, I noticed many cows roaming about. There seemed to be more than the usual amount than I had recently seen in or near New Delhi. I asked my tour guide, "Is it me, or does there appear to be more cows roaming about?" He responded, "Krishna's favorite animal is the cow." I recalled that cows were one of the first domesticated animals known to man and represented the only source of abundant milk for early man's survival. I also noticed that my guide had responded in the present tense. Lord Krishna was still alive in spirit.

Through my guide, I learned that Lord Krishna, who was called Gopal as a child, and his adopted family were cow herders. Hindus believe that many koti spirits (males that take on female identities) live in the cows. Thus, they are considered sacred. This is similar to Christian beliefs, as mutilation, torture, or

Sacred Cow in Mathura, India

Sri Krishna Temple

mistreatment of animals is considered breaking the Christian's fifth Commandment. Because of their holiness, Hindus believe that touching these cows will bring one good luck. Hitting or pushing them will bring one bad luck. Further, Hindus believe that a cow is a perfect animal with four teats: one teat for the calf, one for guests, one for the use of rituals, and one teat for its master. Cows provide milk out of pure love.

As we approached Sri Krishna Bhoomi Temple, I noticed a male baby being carried by his mother. He had dark black coloring under his eyes similar to eyeliner. I asked my tour guide why the baby's eyes were painted. He explained that the coloring is necessary to ward off evil spirits from the baby's sight. As we entered the temple of Krishna's birthplace, I noticed great security. We were body-searched not once, but three times. Because there were only a few visitors that day, we walked in without having to wait in any lines.

Upon arrival into the room where Krishna was born, I witnessed a limestone bed and Krishna's baby picture placed atop the limestone. He resembled a baby cherub but bedazzled with jewels of red rubies, pearls, and diamond earrings, his headdress covered in diamonds and pearls. He is pictured eating something similar to porridge out of an urn and smiling. Lord Krishna lived for 125 years. He is known as the symbol of love. He is the eighth incarnation of Lord Vishnu and was brought to earth to end chaos and evil. The name "Krishna" in Sanskrit means black or dark. Thus, He is often portrayed in a blue hew. According to the Vedas, Lord Krishna is a dark-skinned Dravidian God. Hindus believe that the color blue symbolizes immeasurability and infinity. Thus, what

Lord Krishna

is immeasurable can only be seen in blue to mortal eyes. Hindus celebrate Lord Krishna in a yearly festival called "Janmashtami." In 2018, Lord Krishna's 535th birth anniversary was celebrated. His influential words can be read in the Srimad Bhagavad-Gita, a holy manuscript for Hindus comprising 700 verses originally written in Sanskrit.

Lord Krishna believed that by outwardly performing all actions but inwardly renouncing its fruits, the wise, purified by the fire of transcendental knowledge, attain peace, detachment, forbearance, spiritual vision, and bliss. Lord Krishna is the supreme truth, the supreme cause and sustaining force of everything, both material and spiritual. Advanced souls surrender devotion unto Him, whereas impious souls divert their minds to other objects of worship.

Hindus believe that by remembering Lord Krishna in devotion throughout one's life and especially in the time of death, one can enter His supreme abode, beyond the material world. Because Lord Krishna represents the supreme Godhead and the supreme object of worship, the soul is eternally related to Him through transcendental devotional service (bhakti). By reviving one's pure devotion, one returns to Lord Krishna in the spiritual realm.

As I looked at this holy birthplace, I recalled my 2015 visit to Jesus' birthplace in Bethlehem, which was more than emotional. Jesus' birthplace felt ethereal. I could not believe that I was actually touching his birthplace, the actual spot wherein the Virgin Mary gave birth to Jesus Christ, the redeemer of the world, an event still celebrated by Christians all over the world. I remembered the powerful words in John 1:14, KJV: "And the Word was made flesh." This visit not only reinforced the significance of the birth of my God, but I also understood the crucial importance of other gods such as Lord Krishna and that this site and event are also salient and valid.

Standing in Krishna's Holy birthplace, my memory transported me to the edicule, the tomb of Jesus in Jerusalem. Perhaps the similar limestone bed that both Jesus and Lord Krishna rested on prompted my memory. Upon seeing the limestone bed in 2015 when I visited Jerusalem, I could not help but feel spellbound and transfixed at this holy and historical sight. I did not want to leave. I felt lamentation but also pride and happiness. In this temple, I felt the same. The only difference: I did not feel the same for me. Instead, I felt lamentation, pride and happiness for the Hindus for having such a powerful Lord. I bought a small oval picture of Lord Krishna as a child. It hangs next to the image of Jesus in my home altar. The bible passage that came to my mind at this moment was, "Behold, a virgin shall be with child, and shall bring forth a son, and they shall call his name Emmanuel, which being interpreted is, God with us" (Matthew 1:23 AKJV).

After having a lunch of dal, roti, and fresh vegetables, we continued our sojourn to Chhatarpur Temple, located in South Delhi. The second-largest Hindu temple in New Delhi, it is dedicated to the Goddess Durga. There are multi buildings within this temple. One can experience a soulful presence in this temple sprawling with well-kept lush gardens. The name Durga in Sanskrit means "fortress" or a place that is difficult to overrun. This Goddess represents the protective mother of the universe and appears in many female forms. One of Hinduism's most popular deities, Durga protects all that is good and harmonious. She can appear as having multiple limbs and fighting evil. Her other avatars include Kali, Bhagvati, Ambika, Lalita, and Java. At times, Durga may appear as more than one avatar at a time.

She is the protectress of humanity. She is invoked by devotees to end the misery in a person's life. She also cleans a person's

Chhatarpur Temple

spirit of negativity such as hatred, anger, jealousy, and selfishness. Sometimes, Durga is gentle in her approach, but not always. Her images are almost always beautiful and adorned in red, which symbolizes action and activity. She is constantly on the move. Her most prominent feature is Durga's many arms which hold symbolic weapons. She also rides on a powerful tiger or lion. Her weapons

Goddess Durga

include the conch shell which imitates the sound of "ohm." This sound is the word used when God created the universe. Her other weapons are the bow and arrow which represent her limitless energy (potential and kinetic energy); the thunderbolt, which represents her strong conviction and willpower; a half-bloomed lotus, which represents the evolution and potential spirituality and knowledge; the discus, which is above her forefinger but does not touch her forefinger, signifying that the universe is under her control; the sword, which symbolizes a quest for knowledge that will cut through false illusions; and the trident (a three-pronged spear), which symbolizes the three types of misery humanity suffers: the spiritual misery, the physical misery and human's mental misery. Durga's mantra is "Salutations to see who is the most beautiful of the seeker of the truth."

Similar to Hinduism, the Christian Virgin Mother Mary is believed to manifest her beauty in many forms, such as Our Lady of Loreto and Our Lady of Guadalupe, and in many places such as Fatima in Portugal, Bosnia, and Lourdes, and even in Kerala, India, located in the Malabar Coast of India. She also has many churches named in her honor. Like Mother Mary, Durga serves as the protector of all humans, watching over humanity with great and tender motherly care.

After visiting the beautiful Chhatarpur Temple and learning about many deities and goddesses and their magnificent history, we walked across the street to the Lord Hanuman Red Statue. Lord Hanuman is better known as the monkey-faced Lord. Lord Hanuman is a devotee of Lord Rama and represents great strength and courage and is the reincarnation of Lord Shiva. Hanuman, one of the most celebrated Lords in Hindu mythology, was born in Mount Sumeru, a five peaked mountain, also known as Mount Meru in the Himalayas. His parents were Vayu (father, the wind god) and Anjana (mother).

    According to my tour guide, Mr. Rana, the red Hanuman Statue Temple is the tallest Hanuman statue in the world. It is difficult to approach it as there are several very busy streets to maneuver around at the entrance of this temple. Once inside, we entered a darkened cave-like atmosphere. This inner sanctum had various twists and turns; we witnessed the life of Lord Hanuman depicted through colorful staged scenes with smaller statues; we also saw mother Goddess Anjana Devi, Lord Hanuman's mother. The construction of this temple began in the 10th century.

    After visiting this impressive temple, we visited the Monkey Temple. Officially this temple is called *Galtaji*. It is located in Jaipur in the state of Rajasthan. The macaque monkeys that reside at this temple are considered sacred; thus, they are not allowed to be touched; they represent Lord Hanuman (Hanuman in Sanskrit means *disfigured jaw*). Some Hindus believe the macaque monkeys that reside in and around this temple are distant cousins of Lord Hanuman. The guide and caregiver of this temple was a young

Hanuman Temple

Galtaji Temple (The Monkey Temple)

man about seventeen years old. When we arrived, we walked up a small hill where the temple stood. The monkeys stood outside the temple as if ready to greet their visitors. There were approximately 30 monkeys of all ages. As the young guide escorted us up the zig-zagging hill, the monkeys approached us; they included infants, adolescents, and larger-sized adults. We offered them chocolate candy and peanuts. They eagerly grabbed them and quickly ran away. Upon seeing the male monkeys get closer to us, our guide scared them away. I asked why he did that; he explained that the male monkeys are too aggressive with fellow monkeys and humans alike. Our guide repeatedly reminded me not to touch the holy monkeys.

Next, we continued to a place where I wanted to see and maybe ride an elephant. I wanted to see how the Hindu treated and reacted to elephants because I knew that elephants represented Lord Ganesh, whose father is Lord Shiva and mother is Parvati and has an elephant head, make him easy to identify. Lord Ganesh represents the remover

Representation of Lord Ganesh

of obstacles, the patron of science and art, and, also, intelligence and wisdom. We arrived at the Elephant Conservation and Care Center. I had never ridden on an elephant, and I was excited to do so. At this elephant rehabilitation center, one notices the great passion, love, and great reverence the caregivers had for each elephant. I got an opportunity to not only ride on an elephant but also feed one which is said to bring good luck to the person feeding them. Once on the elephant, I felt the great gentle glide stemming from its large feet that gently touched the ground. The ride felt as though I was on a cloud—the smoothest ride I had ever felt. The tremendous care for these revered elephants impressed me the most about this center.

Venerated Elephants in India

After the elephant conservation and care center, we continued our sojourn to the Jama Masjid, one of the largest mosques in India, located in Chandni Chowk, a busy shopping area. India is home to the third-largest Muslim population, constituting approximately 10% of India's total population. Islam was brought to India in the ninth century by Arabian and Persians. While not a Hindu

Jama Mosque

temple, I nonetheless stood awed by its tremendous immensity. Its vastness reminded me of my God's great importance in my life and of what my mother would always tell her children, "Dios es muy grande" (God is very big). This was a phrase I would never forget and later took as my own with a slight rephrasing: "God is much, much more powerful than we as humans can ever imagine."

I wore short pants that day, so I had to cover my legs before my entrance. The guard at the entrance provided me a lungi (skirt) to wear over my shorts so that I may cover my legs. As I walked around the vastness of this alluring mosque, I noticed the worshippers stopped to stare at my lungi (skirt). I could not understand why they were staring because other men wore similar skirts. Perhaps I wore it differently. I was not sure.

As I continued sauntering around this beautiful and peaceful place, I could not help but notice its ornate Islamic architecture of onion-shaped copulas and minarets from where a muezzin or crier calls the faithful to prayer. We climbed this narrow minaret and saw New Delhi. As I looked downward, I noticed a public bus driving by the mosque and people tossing coins toward the mosque. Mr. Rana explained that tossing money to the mosque is a custom for devout Muslims. The money is used for charity, schools, the homeless, the poor, and hospitals. Charity contribution is an obligation for all Muslims.

As I roamed about in this prodigious place, I thought about how much more manageable a monotheistic belief in one God was to understand and practice. I also felt a strong connection to Muslims for this. The commonality of Muslims' devotion to Allah was very similar to my Christian belief in one God. I felt the "simplicity" of worshiping only one God. Although there were hundreds of people at this mosque, there existed a great peacefulness and dynamic solace.

Pagal Baba Temple was our next visit on this day. Located in Vrindavan, Uttar Pradesh, this eleven-story white marble structure is the domain of Lord Krishna. Hindus believe that Lord Krishna spent his youth here. This modern temple houses robotic puppets and dioramas which depict important events in India history, the life of Rama, and the life of Lord Krishna. You can also view the city of Vrindavan from the top floor. This temple was built in 1947 by a wealthy man named Pagal Baba who was a devout follower of Lord Krishna and also had his own followers. He wanted to use his inherited wealth to honor Lord Krishna through the construction of this magnificent and beautiful temple. Upon Pagal Baba's death, his followers continued the construction of this temple until its completion in 1977.

> *"Honour the Lord with thy substance, and with the firstfruits of all thine increase" (Proverbs 3:9 AKJV).*

Pagal Baba Temple

IX

St. Anthony's Secondary School

"An ignorant man is lost, faithless, and filled with self-doubt" (Bhagavad-Gita).

Day 9

Today was going to be a day "free" of temples. I merely wanted to walk around and enjoy the day. After walking for only two blocks, I ran into a school playground. As a teacher of more than twenty years, I can usually look at children and correctly determine what grade they are in. From the playground gate, I could tell the all-male children were in middle school grades. They were playing cricket. The British brought cricket to India in the 17th century and is still very popular today. I decided to take a look inside and see the learning environment in the school. When I finally found the entrance, I noticed its name: St. Anthony's Boys Secondary School. St. Anthony was born Fernando Marins de Bulhoes in Lisbon, Portugal. He was a Catholic priest and friar of the Franciscan order. He is said to be the patron saint of lost and stolen articles.

Christianity is said to have begun in India by Thomas the apostle who arrived in Kerala in 52 A.D. Today, it is estimated that Catholicism has 20% devotees and Christianity has 28 million followers that constitute 2.3 percent of India's total population and live in 174 dioceses, the largest in Asia.

India was the first Asian country visited by a Pope in the Catholic Church's two millennia of history. Pope Paul VI visited Mumbai in 1964. Later, Pope John visited India twice, in 1986 and 1999. In a letter to the Archbishop of India, Pope John Paul II wrote, "The need for unity and the preservation of diversity must not be interpreted as being against each other" (Espitula ad India Episcipos, May 28, 1987).

At the office, I introduced myself and asked the headmaster for permission to have a tour. He was very welcoming and also informed me that this was an all-male school for orphans. It is estimated that there were twenty-million orphans in India. The literacy rate in India is 74.4%—males at 82% and female literacy at 82.4% (2011 India Census). The state of Kerala is the most literate in India with 94% literacy.

The headmaster agreed that I could take a tour and provided a male guide. The guide took me to eight classrooms. The first classroom was a language class. In all the classrooms, the students immediately stood up as we walked in, as a sign of respect for adults. I met the teachers in each room and introduced myself. The students all wore blue short pants uniforms. The classrooms were bare and had no air conditioning nor fans. The students' and teachers' tables appeared very old. Despite these conditions, they all seemed very happy, continually smiling at me. In this classroom, the students were studying Sanskrit, an ancient language that is over 3,500 years old and once spoken widely in India. Now, Sanskrit is mostly used in religious writings and religious ceremonies and required for high school graduation.

After my visit to St. Anthony's Boys' Secondary School, I thought about the selfless devotion the teachers gave to educate the orphaned children despite the learning/teaching conditions and the extremely bad environment. Yet, every teacher seemed happy to be there as were the students. I felt that the young male students appreciated what the school was doing for them. They knew they were orphans yet were happy and positive. At that moment, as in many moments, I felt deeply proud to be a Christian. The spirit of my Lord abounded in this school. And, many other Lords resided in the children's hearts as well.

> *"The life of the body is the soul, the life of the soul is Christ" (St. Anthony of Padua).*

X

Mother Teresa's Missionaries of Charity Jeevan Jyoti Home

"How can there be too many children? That is like saying there are too many flowers" (Mother Teresa).

Day 10

Today was my last day in India. I could not leave India without visiting Mother Teresa Missionaries of Charity Jeevan Jyoti Home in Jangpura, New Delhi. The Sisters of Charity organization is a Roman Catholic religious congregation established in 1950 by Mother Teresa. She was born in 1910 in Albania and was canonized by Pope Francis in 2016. Mother Teresa was also the recipient of the Nobel Peace Prize. The sisters of this congregation take vows to give wholeheartedly free service to the poorest of the poor. They care for refugees, former prostitutes, the mentally ill, and lepers. In addition to running orphan centers and adult centers for the homeless, they also run many soup kitchens in India and around the world.

The orphanage that I visited was a two-story building that raises orphaned children. On this day, upon meeting the mother superior (she asked to remain anonymous), she informed me that there were currently forty orphans living at this place. She gave me a tour, and I realized that in addition to this being a children's home, it also served as their school. Classrooms were on the first floor and bedrooms were on the second. It was nap time when I arrived; the younger children were asleep in their cribs while the older ones attended classes downstairs. At every room, the mother superior said something kind to the children and waved goodbye at them while also reminding the workers not to forget this or that duty, always with a kind and gentle tone. The children who could not sleep were happy to see her the mother superior. The mother superior informed me that most of their children are females. I asked how she finds them and where they come from. She stated that the local police call them from railroad stations where the children are usually abandoned. Most abandoned children, she added, were females. Many are infants. It is estimated that 90% of abandoned children in India are females.

I asked the mother superior if she ever met Mother Teresa. She said, "Of course. She was the one who trained me." I asked her what was one thing that Mother Teresa taught her. She responded, "She taught me love and compassion." She also added that Mother Teresa visited this place many times.

As we were talking in a small conference room, a middle-aged Indian couple came in. They wanted to give a monetary donation. They explained that their mentally ill female child had recently died. And they wanted to donate to this center because of the love they give to children like their daughter. When they left, I continued my tour with the mother superior. She showed me the playground and her small office. I asked her, "What is the best thing people can do?" She responded, "Love the poor."

"Whosoever therefore shall humble himself as this

little child, the same is greatest in the kingdom of heaven. And whoso shall receive one such little child in my name receiveth me" (Matthew 18:4-5 AKJV).

Conclusion

When I began my religious studies at Southern Methodist University, I began to think about where my God fit into the scheme of the Hindu religion.

I began my journey to India with one question: where was my Jesus and my God within and among the Hindu? One thing is clear: In my sojourn to India, I gained much more than what I gave in my search. From the first day I arrived and did not want to leave my hotel room at the Prime Balaji Deluxe Hotel to my last day in India, I can say that my God was always with me in my heart, in my spirit. Thus, my journey through India and its many holy temples greatly augmented my faith in Jesus, both in depth and breadth. I also found a genuine understanding and respect of and for varied religions. I shy away from using the phrase "other religions" because the word "other" pre-supposes that my religion is most paramount. While it is paramount to me, I am not the only one on this planet.

I learned that, for me, it is extremely crucial to practice Kirtan, a Hindu tradition that values the absolute truth in everyone's heart. This connects us all to the Divine, bringing peace and unity to all the world. Several texts have also furthered my understanding of Hindu and India's past, present, and future. These texts include *The Wonder That Was Ind*ia by A.L. Basham, which is a history of the oldest civilization of India; *The Bhagavad Gita*, the holy book of Hindus; *The Ramayana*, one of the world's oldest pieces of literature, a text of the history of Hindu gods and goddesses and profound philosophy; *Hindu Wisdom for All God's Children;* Gandhi's autobiography, *The Story of My Experiments with Truth*; and *The Bhagavad Gita*, which means "song of God." This song resides in the hearts and spirituality of all humans. This holy book, like the Holy Bible, contains the essence of the purification of humans' souls. Like the Holy Bible, the Gita belongs to all humanity, not only Hindus, just as the Bible belongs to all mankind, not just Christians.

However powerful and filled with spiritual guidance these books are, no amount of reading could have prepared me for the immense dichotomy and holiness that is India and Hinduism in particular. My spiritual sojourn not only reinforced that my Jesus and my God exist everywhere, but also that other gods exist everywhere as well. Why humans believe in different gods is beyond the scope of my knowledge nor is it a question that matters to me. By entertaining this query, I was only creating spiritual blinders and was beginning to see God in one light, from one perspective which was considerably preventing me from seeing and being truly illuminated by the Holy Spirit. "Knowledge can only be got in one way, the way of experience; there is no other way to know" (Swami Vivekananda).

Hinduism taught me the many manifestations of the powerful God. Of the manifestations, Gandhi wrote, "His manifestations are innumerable; they overwhelm me with wonder and awe and for a moment stun me, yet I worship God as truth only." Swami Vivekananda said, "The more religions there are, the more opportunities for making a successful appeal to the divine instinct inside all of us."

God's spiritual demonstration of His protection and guidance proved evident every day while I was in India. His presence was foremost in every temple and the poor. I felt His existence every time I felt scared or perceived confusion or felt dumbfounded. I saw the beauty of His benevolence. I heard the thunderous power of His silence. In short, I have come to understand God's beautiful "otherness."

What I learned to admire most about Hinduism is how its followers proudly display their beliefs with outward displays of small and large amulets and body gestures; for example, many Hindus wear colorful amulets around their necks, their lapels; they display talismans on their vehicles' front console, on antennas, on their motor vehicles' side mirrors, and on mopeds. Hindus openly greet each other with a blessing known as "Namaste," a customary greeting of a slight bow and hands pressed together, palms gently touching and fingers pointing upward. Namaste is used for both greetings and departures and signifies love for the soul and spirit residing within each of us. This greeting greatly reminds me of my Mexican heritage where a person's departures are often accompanied with religious farewells such as "adios" (to God I send you), "que Dios te bendiga" (God bless you), and "Vaya con Dios" (go with God). Many times, the sign of the holy Christian trinity is made in front of the departing person's face. Contrastingly, my American culture's outward display of religion is often frowned upon. This is neither good nor bad. It is just part and parcel of different cultural norms. As a Mexican American, I have learned to adjust to the accepted customs depending on my surroundings and whom I am in the company of. Like Hindus, I vowed to celebrate my Catholicism. "Religion is the manifestation of Divinity already in man" (Swami Vivekananda).

In my pilgrimage to India, I observed that God has many beautiful lights that transcend even their own radiance and luminescence. He is in every place that you look because you are looking for and with His eyes. Similar to Catholic saints born in India, such as St. Gonzalo Garcia, born of a Portuguese father and Indian mother, St. Joseph Vaz, St. Euphrasia, St. Alphonsa, and St. Kuriakose Chavara, many Hindu deities, who for many centuries, have performed miracles, lived virtuous lives and are venerated for their goodness. In India, I witnessed that God's sacred words represent more than mere letters on a page. The word of God is also found in India's sacred traditions. For it is these sacred traditions that mostly project themselves in Hinduism. Perhaps it is these traditions that serve as its catalyst and genesis for its historical survival.

In my spiritual sojourn to India, I also learned that I needed to find ways to enrich my faith by looking outward and by not disparaging other faiths, for that was my charge. The Dalai Lama (Lhamo Dondrub) once said that India was the best example of religious tolerance, where non-violence and religious harmony was propagated as early as 3,000 years ago. When I was a child, I recall asking my father, Pedro Chavez, who had served in World War II, "Dad, what if there is no Jesus, no God of any kind?" He responded, "I believe that what matters most is that we love each other as humans no matter where we are from or what we believe."

In my pilgrimage, I learned that being Catholic, like being Hindu, takes considerable courage. I regained my strength and courage from Hindus' steadfastness, allegiance, constancy, and fidelity. Although Catholics receive much criticism from non-Catholics for worshipping saints as opposed to only having one God (a false stereotype), I have been rededicated to my Catholicism. I not only gained strength by Hindus' examples of devotion, but I also re-learned that Jesus was my strength indeed. "I will love Thee, O Lord, my strength" (Psalms 18:1, AKJV). In a visit to Paris' Notre Dame Cathedral, Gandhi wrote:

> *Kneeling and praying to the saints could not be mere superstition. The devotees' souls kneeling before the Virgin could not be worshipping mere marble. They were fired with genuine devotion and they worship not stone but the divinity of what it was symbolic of. By this worship, they were not detracting but increasing the Glory of God (The Stories of my Experiments with Truth. Audiobook 2009).*

Most of all, my pilgrimage taught me that "You have to grow from the inside out. No one can make you spiritual. There is no other teacher but your own soul" (Swami Vivekananda).

The examples provided by Hindus' devoted love and loyalty to their varied holy lords and gods deeply resonated in my heart, my mind, and my future actions. I digested the fact that Catholic (which means 'that which comes from the whole') is merely a small, yet very important part, of the "whole" world of believers. I must continue to expand my knowledge of other religions to continue to enrich my own conviction. For many years, I heard of Christians taking pilgrimages to Fatima in Northern Portugal, Avila in Spain, Guadalupe in Mexico, or Lourdes in France as well as Galilee, Jerusalem, and Bethlehem. Because of my pilgrimage to India, I can now look forward to making more pilgrimages to the aforementioned holy places. In doing so, I can more readily understand God's significance. Similarly, I look forward to making pilgrimages to Japan to discover Buddhism, to Mecca to discover Islam in more depth, to Central America to study the beliefs of the Aztec and Mayan gods, and the places whence my culture derives.

"I will be glad and rejoice in Thee: I will sing praise to thy name, O Lord most High" (Psalm 9:2 AKJV).

Namaste!

About the Author

Cescilio Chavez is a first-generation American born in San Antonio, Texas. His father was from Mexico, and his mother was from the United States. He is a first-year Seminarian at Southern Methodist University's Perkins School of Theology in Dallas, Texas. He holds an M.A. in Literature from St. Mary's University in San Antonio, Texas and an M. Ed. and Ph.D. in School Administration and Leadership Studies from Our Lady of The Lake Catholic University in San Antonio, Texas. He has served as a public school administrator in San Antonio, Texas as well as the City University of Seattle. He is an educator in Dallas, Texas, where he teaches high school English at the Dallas Independent School District.

He has served as an adjunct professor of Education, writing and American Literature at the University of the Incarnate Word, Wiley College, San Antonio College, Palo Alto College and St. Philip's College. He currently teaches as an adjunct professor of writing and American Literature at El Centro College in Dallas, Texas.

Works Consulted

- Bhaktivedanta Swami Prabhupada, A.C. (1983). *Bhagavad Gita As It Is*: The Bhaktivedanta Book Trust.
- Basham, A. L. (2004). *The Wonder That Was India: A Survey of the History and Culture of the Indian Sub-Continent Before the Coming of the Muslims*: Picador Publishing.
- Clooney S. J., Francis X. (1998). *Hindu Wisdom for All God's Children*: Wipf and Stock Publishers.
- Gandhi, Mohandas K. (2009). *The Stories of My Experiments with Truth (Audiobook):* Blackstone Publishing.
- Malkovsky, Bradley. (2012). *God's Other Children: Personal Encounters with Faith, Love, and Holiness in Sacred India*: HarperOne Publishing.
- Pattanaik, Devdutt. (2012). *Seven Secrets of Shiva (audiobook)*: Westland.
- Dharma, Krishna. (2016). *Ramayana: Retold*: Om Books International.
- *The Ganges: The Devine River*: Video. (2012). Kultur. www.kultur.com.
- *The Holy Bible: Old and New Testament. Authorized King James Version*. (2003). Thomas Nelson Incorporated.
- Vivekananda, Swami. (2013). *Complete Works of Swami Vivekananda*. BZ editores.

www.ingramcontent.com/pod-product-compliance
Lightning Source LLC
Chambersburg PA
CBHW042232090526
44587CB00006B/153